D1228827

DISCOVER
ANCIENT
ROME

DISCOVER ANCIENT CIVILIZATIONS

DISCOVER
ANCIENT
ROME

Deborah Kops

 Enslow Publishers, Inc.
40 Industrial Road
Box 398
Berkeley Heights, NJ 07922
USA

http://www.enslow.com

North Sea

Baltic Sea

Britannia

Germania
Inferior

Moesia
Superior

Atlantic
Ocean

Belgica

Panonia
Superior

Panonia
Inferior

Lugdunensis

Germania
Superior

Raetia

Noricum

Dacia

Bay of Biscay

Aquitania

Narbonensis

Italia

Illyricum

Adriatic Sea

Tarraconensis

Alps

Corsica

Rome

Macedonia

Lusitania

Sardinia

Bactica

Epirus

Achaea

Mauretania
Caesariensis

Mediterranean Sea

Mauretania
Tingitana

Africa

Cyrenaica

The Roman Republic at 100 B.C.

The Early Roman Empire at A.D. 14

The Roman Empire at its height in A.D. 116

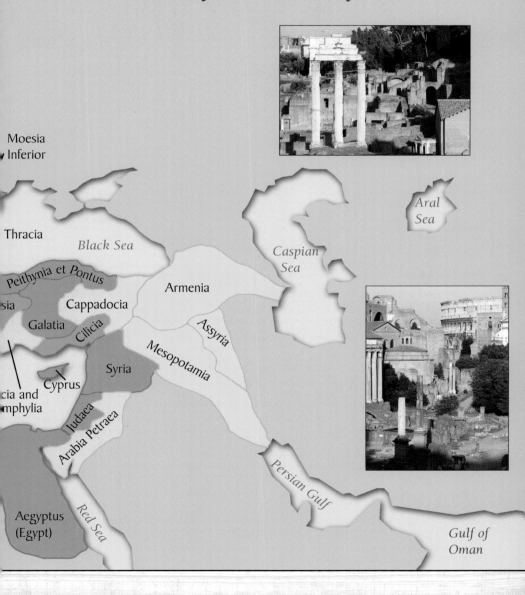

Ancient Rome
1st Century B.C. — 2nd Century A.D.

Moesia
Inferior

Aral
Sea

Thracia

Black Sea

Caspian
Sea

Peithynia et Pontus

Armenia

...sia

Cappadocia

Galatia

Cilicia

Assyria

Mesopotamia

Cyprus

Syria

...cia and
...mphylia

Judaea

Arabia Petraea

Persian Gulf

Aegyptus
(Egypt)

Red Sea

Gulf of
Oman

This book previously published as *Ancient Rome* in 2005.

Library of Congress Cataloging-in-Publication Data:

Kops, Deborah.
  Discover Ancient Rome / Deborah Kops.
    p. cm. — (Discover ancient civilizations)
  Includes bibliographical references and index.
  Summary: "Learn about the art and cultural contributions, family life, religions and people of ancient
Rome"—Provided by publisher.
  ISBN 978-0-7660-4199-8
  1. Rome—Civilization—Juvenile literature. I. Title.
  DG77.K68 2014
  937—dc23
                            2012011576

Future editions:
Paperback ISBN 978-1-4644-0341-5   Multi-user PDF 978-0-7660-5819-4
ePUB ISBN 978-1-4645-1190-5   Single-user PDF 978-1-4646-1190-2

Printed in the United States of America

102013 Lake Book Manufacturing, Inc., Melrose Park, IL

10 9 8 7 6 5 4 3 2 1

To Our Readers: We have done our best to make sure all Internet Addresses in this book were active
and appropriate when we went to press. However, the author and the publisher have no control over
and assume no liability for the material available on those Internet sites or on other Web sites they may
link to. Any comments or suggestions can be sent by e-mail to comments@enslow.com or to the
address on the back cover.

Every effort has been made to locate all copyright holders of material used in this book. If any errors or
omissions have occurred, corrections will be made in future editions of this book.

♻ Enslow Publishers, Inc., is committed to printing our books on recycled paper. The paper in every
book contains 10% to 30% post-consumer waste (PCW). The cover board on the outside of each
book contains 100% PCW. Our goal is to do our part to help young people and the environment too!

Photo Credits: ©2012 Photos.com, a division of Getty Images. All rights reserved., pp. 26-27, 44, 55,
66-67; ©Clipart.com/2012 Photos.com, a division of Getty Images. All rights reserved., pp. 13, 22, 41,
52-53, 78, 81(top), 92; ©Corel Corporation, pp. 5, 11, 19, 33, 50-51, 68, 77, 81(bottom), 83;
©Enslow Publishers, Inc., pp. 4-5, 62; grafalex/©2012 Photos.com, a division of Getty Images. All
rights reserved., pp. 42-43; J. Scott Applewhite/AP Images, p. 91; JupiterImages/©2012 Photos.com, a
division of Getty Images. All rights reserved., p. 38; manuel velasco /2012 Photos.com, a division of
Getty Images. All rights reserved., p. 24; Massimo Merlini//©2012 Photos.com, a division of Getty
Images. All rights reserved., pp. 94-95; Shutterstock.com, pp. 15, 30-31, 72-73, 85, 86, 97, 98;
Wikipedia.com public domain image, p. 65.

Front Cover: Background: Coliseum(grafalex/©2012 Photos.com, a division of Getty Images. All
rights reserved.); Foreground: Statue of Augustus(©Corel Corporation)

Table of CONTENTS

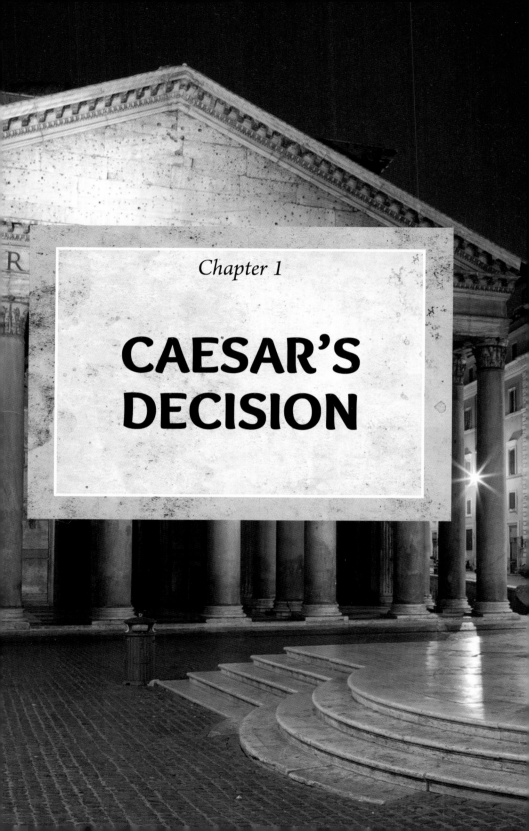

Chapter 1

CAESAR'S DECISION

In January 49 B.C., the Roman general Julius Caesar had to make a difficult choice. His command as governor and head of the armies in Gaul (what is today France and Belgium) was officially coming to an end. The Roman Senate, the governing body made up of members of Rome's leading families, demanded that Caesar give up his armies there and return to the city of Rome. This tall, fair-skinned man was a military hero and one of the most powerful men in the Roman Empire. At the time, Rome was stronger than any other power in Europe. Greece, once the brightest political star in the ancient Mediterranean world, had become a Roman province.

A few years before Caesar faced his difficult decision, Caesar's rival, Pompey, had become extremely powerful in Rome's government. A struggle between Caesar and Pompey grew, and now the Senate decided

Julius Caesar was one of ancient Rome's greatest generals, and his leadership inspired the loyalty of the men in his command.

to show its support for Pompey by demanding that Caesar leave his army in Gaul. Caesar knew that if he did as the Senate asked and crossed the Rubicon River between Gaul and Italy without his army, his political career would likely be over.[1] Or he could ignore the Senate's demand, bring his army into Italy, and challenge Pompey for the leadership of the empire.

Caesar and Pompey had not always been rivals. Caesar's daughter, Julia, was Pompey's wife, and ten years earlier, they had shared the rule of Rome with a third man for one year in what was known as the First Triumvirate. When their terms as leaders were over, Caesar was appointed military commander and governor of the Roman province that included northern Italy and southern Gaul. Pompey, with the support of the Senate, became sole consul, or chief magistrate, the most powerful member of government.

According to legend, as Caesar crossed the Rubicon, he cried out, "Let the dice fly high!"

Crossing the Rubicon

Julius Caesar was not content to quietly rule his province, however.[2] Instead, he took his army into central and then northern Gaul. For eight years, this dedicated, energetic general and his army fought the independent peoples of Gaul until they conquered all of Gaul for the Roman Empire. The Romans were the first people in the ancient world to train and keep professionally trained army, and Caesar's campaigns proved his military genius. Caesar also found the time to write a dramatic account of his victories, *Commentaries on the Gallic War*, which contributed to his fame and glory.

On January 10, 49 B.C., Caesar made the decision to enter Italy with his men. According to legend, as he crossed the Rubicon with his army, he cried out, "Let the dice fly high!"[3] He was hoping that fate

These Roman soldiers show typical military equipment: shields, spears, plumed helmets, bronze breastplates, and greaves (armor that protected the soldier's shins). Originally the Roman army was made up of volunteers, but by the time of Julius Caesar soldiers had become full-time paid professionals.

would be kind to him, just as people do when they throw dice in a game. And he was willing to accept the consequences of his decision. As it turned out, the consequences were enormous: Caesar's decision, which thrust the Roman Empire into civil war, changed the course of Roman history.

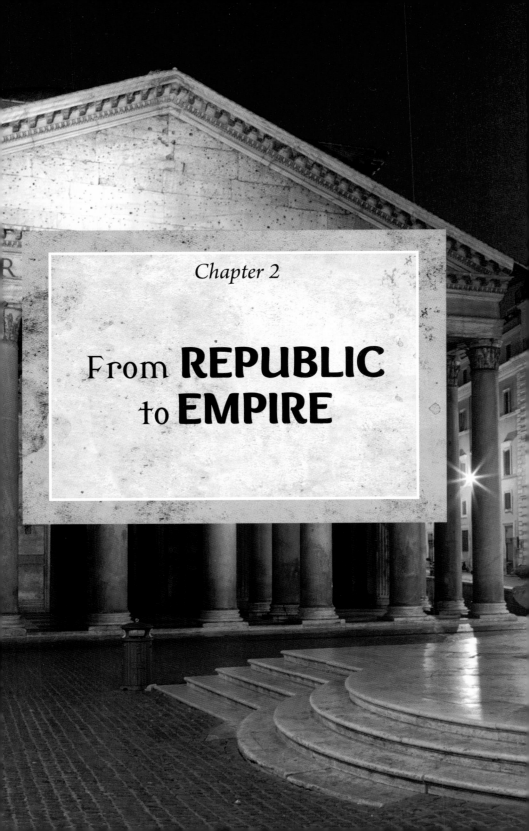

Chapter 2

From REPUBLIC to EMPIRE

For a year and a half, Julius Caesar and Pompey fought for leadership of the Roman Empire, plunging it into a civil war. In a remarkable series of military campaigns, Caesar defeated Pompey's armies in Italy and in Spain, which was part of the empire, and forced Pompey to flee to Greece.[1] There on June 6, 48 B.C., the two armies fought their final battle in Pharsalus, in northern Greece. That battle proved to be Caesar's greatest victory against Pompey who fled the battlefield and escaped to Egypt.

Caesar's Brief Rule

When Pompey arrived in Egypt, however, he was murdered on the orders of the pharaoh. Even without Pompey, Caesar continued to meet with resistance. It took him until October, 45 B.C. to destroy his remaining enemies in Macedonia, a kingdom north of Greece; Asia Minor, the

By 45 B.C., Julius Caesar had created the strongest army in the ancient world. One year later, he declared himself dictator of Rome for life—but his life would soon come to an end.

GIVLIO CESARE

peninsula between the Black Sea and the Aegean Sea that is today part of Turkey; and Spain.

By then, Caesar had created the strongest and most effective army in the world.[2] But he also was smart enough to realize that he would need the support of the many people he had just conquered if his rule was to be effective. The Roman historian Velleius Paterculus (c. 19 B.C. to A.D. 32) described Caesar's great triumph as well as his generosity: "Victorious over all his enemies, Caesar returned to Rome and, a thing incredible, pardoned all who had borne arms against him."[3]

Dictator for Life

The great Roman general was hungry for political power as well as military power. In 44 B.C., he appointed himself dictator for life and began appearing in public on a gold-covered chair, as if he were king.

His actions angered the members of Rome's most prominent families, who had shared power with the country's leader through political appointments and by serving in the Senate. Even though Caesar had brought about reforms and helped to secure the vast reaches of the empire, critics resented his power. They also wanted to maintain the empire's democracy, and they were afraid that Caesar would destroy it. On March 15, in 44 B.C., men who had once been his friends stabbed Julius Caesar to death in a public theater where the Senate had chosen to meet.

Caesar was fifty-five years old when he was murdered. One of the most talented men to lead ancient Rome, he was a superb military commander and a gifted writer. But he also helped to destroy Rome's republican form of government, which had lasted for five hundred years.[4]

Julius Caesar was assassinated by men who once had been his friends on March 15, 44 B.C.

The Early Years of the Republic

The ancient Romans created a legend to explain the birth of their country. It begins with Aeneas, the Trojan hero already a part of Greek mythology. In order to escape the destruction of the city of Troy, Aeneas flees to Italy. There he begins a family line that will eventually produce kings. The twin brothers from the family, Romulus and Remus, are abandoned on the banks of the Tiber River, which runs through Rome. The twins are rescued by a she-wolf and helped by a shepherd. Later the brothers argue, and Romulus kills Remus. Romulus eventually founds the city of Rome on the banks of the Tiber, where he had been rescued.

People have been living in the low hills surrounding Rome since at least the tenth or eleventh century B.C. By the seventh century B.C., Rome was an established city-state, which consisted of the city and the surrounding region. For a time, it was ruled by Etruscan kings from Etruria, to the north. The Etruscans were a powerful people. Under their leadership, Rome was expanding its territory and developing a warlike culture.

Discover Ancient Rome

The legend of Rome's founding is the subject of this sculpture, which shows the wolf that rescued the twin brothers, Romulus and Remus.

In 509 B.C., the Romans rebelled and exiled the last Etruscan king, Tarquin the Proud, and founded a republic.[5] Under a government led by two elected consuls and the Senate, the Romans enlarged their empire by conquering their neighbors. By about 270 B.C., the Romans controlled the entire Italian penisula and were ready to challenge the other powers on the Mediterranean Sea.

The Struggle Between Rome and Carthage

In 218 B.C., Rome clashed with Carthage, an empire on the north African coast, southeast of Italy, for the second time in about forty years. The problem began when Carthage was looking to expand its territory westward into Spain. The Romans challenged the aggressive move by the Carthaginians and war soon erupted.

The Etruscans, who once ruled Rome, strongly influenced early Roman culture. This sarcophagus, a stone coffin embellished by sculpture, is an example of the Etruscans' magnificent artistry.

Rome's north African enemy sent Hannibal, a young and fiery military commander, to invade Italy. Hannibal went on an extraordinary six-month march from Spain to Italy, crossing the Alps with over twenty thousand men, six thousand cavalry (soldiers on horseback), and a small herd of war elephants.[6] Long considered one of the greatest military figures of history, Hannibal defeated Roman armies in Italy that were much greater in number. But the Romans continued to battle Hannibal and his army for over a decade. Then in 202 B.C., the great Roman commander, Publius Scipio, led an army to Africa, forcing Hannibal to leave Italy and defend Carthage. Scipio's army delivered a final crushing blow at the Battle of Zama, defeating Carthage for good. Rome was now master of the western Mediterranean world.

Rome Conquers the Eastern Mediterranean

During the next few decades, Rome sent its armies eastward. By 168 B.C., Rome had conquered Macedonia. In 146, Corinth, an important commercial center of Greece, led a revolt to protest Rome's growing power in its region. The Romans destroyed that great city and made Greece a province of Rome. Almost a century later, before Pompey and Caesar plunged Rome into civil war, Pompey pushed the boundaries of the empire even farther east to include Judaea and the former kingdom of Syria.

The Reign of Augustus

The first emperor of Rome was the great-nephew of Julius Caesar, whom Caesar had adopted as a son. He was later called Augustus, Latin for "respected," but his given name was Octavian. Although Octavian was only eighteen when Caesar

Hannibal famously led an army of war elephants across the Alps—although unfortunately most of them perished in the harsh conditions. The Romans had developed effective tactics against the elephants, leading to Hannibal's defeat at his final battle of Zama in 202 B.C. His elephant charge was ineffective because the disciplined Roman tactical units simply made way for them to pass.

was killed, he was ambitious. By the time Octavian was twenty-one, he began sharing the leadership of the empire with Marc Antony, who had been Caesar's main commander. Together they destroyed the armies of those who had killed Caesar. But by 34 B.C., Antony and Octavian were rivals. Antony had a powerful ally on his side—Cleopatra, the queen of Egypt, who was Antony's lover.

In 31 B.C. when Antony and Cleopatra moved troops to Greece, Octavian, leading the Roman forces, trapped them at Actium, a strip of land off the coast of Greece. Antony and Cleopatra fled to Egypt and, deciding that they were doomed, they killed themselves. Octavian was now the leader of Rome. Within a year, that empire included Egypt. Rome now commanded the lands of the Mediterranean and the Middle East.

In this famous statue of Augustus, the creator of the *Pax Romana*, stands in a triumphant pose like one often used in sculptures of great athletes. This statue was made during his reign.

By 27 B.C. Octavian had establish himself as *imperator*, Latin for commander of all armies. Two years later, the Senate gave Octavian the title *Augustus*, meaning "His Sacred Majesty." The Roman Empire now had an emperor. Many historians view this moment as the end of the Republic and the beginning of the Roman Empire.

Pax Romana

Remembering Caesar's fate, Augustus, the Roman Empire's first emperor, treated the members of the Senate with respect, giving them the impression that he shared power with them. Although power was never returned to the people as it had been during the days of the Republic, Augustus accomplished a great deal during his reign. He granted the provinces local control and allowed different ethnic groups to practice their own customs. He improved the network of roads within the empire and taxed

Rome's citizens more fairly. A period called the *Pax Romana*, or Roman peace, began with Augustus' reign and continued for nearly two hundred years. During this time Roman culture flourished as it spread.

Trajan Stretches the Empire

The Roman Empire reached its greatest size under the emperor Trajan's rule, from A.D. 98 to 117. An experienced army commander, Trajan liked the action of the battlefield. In 106, he conquered Dacia, north of the Danube River, in what is now Romania. Farther east, Trajan won Armenia from the Parthians, leaders of the Persian Empire, in 114. From there his army conquered northern Mesopotamia (present-day Iraq) and advanced all the way to the Persian Gulf. This adventurous emperor's conquests were celebrated by Rome, where the 100-foot-high marble Trajan's Column was built to honor him.

Not every Roman citizen benefited from the enlarged empire, though. Many gave up small farms to serve in the army. When they returned from war, they moved to a city and joined a growing population of poor people. Others had trouble paying the taxes that were used to support Rome's military operations.

Hadrian Strengthens the Borders

Hadrian, the emperor who ruled after Trajan, realized that the endless borders of the enormous Roman Empire had become difficult to defend. To strengthen the places where he thought Rome might be attacked by its enemies, he added permanent bases for the army. His most famous work on the frontier became known as Hadrian's Wall. In 122, Hadrian had this 73-mile (118-kilometer) fortified wall built across the northern border of Roman Britain to keep out the barbarian tribes beyond.

A tall and elegant man with a full beard, Hadrian was a practical ruler. He concentrated on helping the government work more smoothly and gave the Romans two decades of peace before he died in 138.

For the rest of the second century, Rome continued to prosper in the hands of the capable emperors Antoninus Pius and Marcus Aurelius. The Roman army spread Roman culture throughout the empire, encouraging even those in the far reaches of the empire to live as Romans did. In this way, the people in lands that had been conquered by Rome came to feel like Romans themselves. By 212, all free people living in the empire, which stretched from Britain in the west to Arabia in the east, were granted citizenship. But during the third century, the Roman Empire had begun to decline as civil wars, invasions, and economic problems threatened its prosperity and security.

Modern-day view of Hadrian's Wall. The emperor Hadrian strengthened the borders of the empire by stationing military garrisons on its frontiers. Hadrian's Wall, built across Britain's northern border, is the longest surviving Roman structure.

Diocletian Reorganizes the Empire

When Diocletian came to power, in 284, the empire was in need of reorganizing.[7] During the half century before his rule, there had been at least twenty emperors, and many of them had died violently. Still more violence erupted on Rome's borders. Germanic tribes in the north threatened to invade the empire. In the east, the Sassanid people of Persia took Mesopotamia, and the Dacians won their independence.

To help bring stability, Diocletian divided the Roman Empire into eastern and western regions and appointed three men to help him run it. Diocletian also doubled the number of provinces in order to make it easier to collect taxes. In 305, when he was in poor health, he officially gave up his position as emperor.

Constantine Builds a New Capital

A power struggle followed Diocletian's rule. The winner was Constantine, who became the sole ruler of a reunited empire in 324. He was a very forceful leader who broke with tradition in two important ways. First, he embraced and encouraged the spread of Christianity throughout the empire, even though he continued to tolerate other beliefs. Second, in 330 he moved the empire's capital from Rome east to Byzantium, an ancient city later renamed Constantinople in his honor. (It is now Istanbul, Turkey.)

Constantine's peaceful reign saw the building of Christian churches throughout the empire, from Rome to Jerusalem. The emperor also rebuilt the capital, which was near important trade routes and was easy to defend against Rome's Persian enemies to the east.

This map shows the lands that were part of the vast Roman Empire between 44 B.C. to A.D. 180.

The End of the Roman Empire

After Constantine's death in 337, Germanic tribes from the north continued to threaten the empire. To make matters even worse, the relationship between the eastern and western regions of the empire began to break down. This was more serious for the west because the east was much wealthier

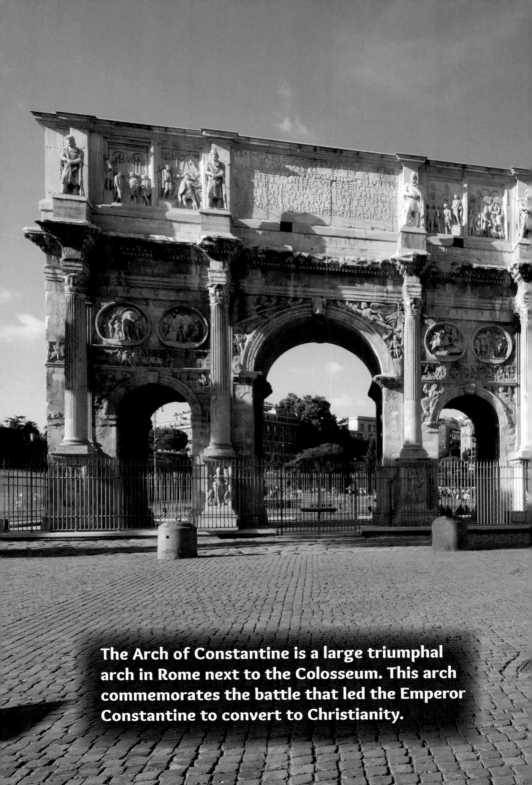

The Arch of Constantine is a large triumphal arch in Rome next to the Colosseum. This arch commemorates the battle that led the Emperor Constantine to convert to Christianity.

Constantine (left) became the emperor of a reunited Roman Empire in A.D. 324 and moved the empire's capital east. Diocletian (right) divided the Roman Empire into eastern and western regions.

and contributed more in support of the empire. In 395, the empire split in two when the emperor Theodosius died. Each region had its own emperor.

In 439, one Germanic tribe, the Vandals, captured the city of Carthage on the coast of north Africa and established the first independent kingdom inside of the empire. By 475, the Goths, another Germanic tribe, had created a kingdom in Gaul and Spain. The next year, German troops who had lived among the Romans and fought in their army suddenly revolted and elected a man named Odoacer as their leader. He made Italy his kingdom, bringing the western half of the Roman Empire to an end. The year 476 has come to signify the fall of the Roman Empire.

Although the Roman government had been toppled, the churches helped to pre-serve Roman culture and offer some pro-tection to the Roman people. The eastern half of the empire, which became known as the Byzantine Empire, lasted until 1453. It survived by bargaining with its enemies and integrating them into the empire instead of fighting them.[8]

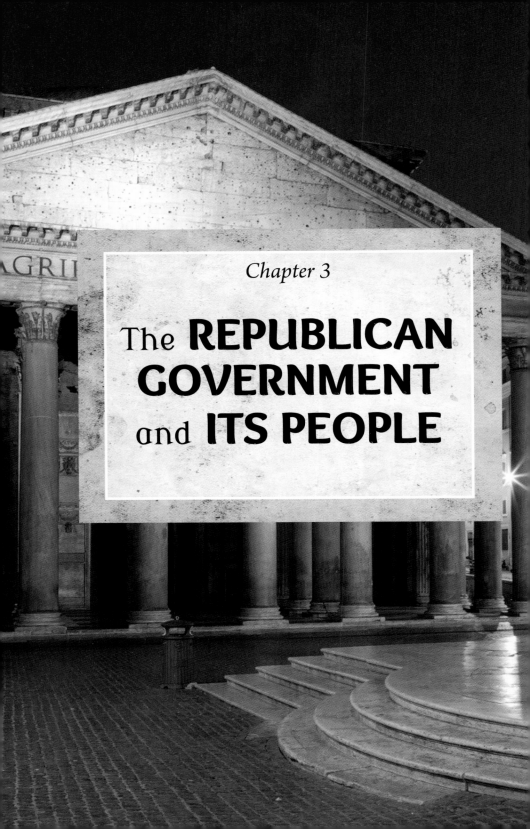

Chapter 3

The REPUBLICAN GOVERNMENT and ITS PEOPLE

From the earliest days of the Republic, a person's social class affected his ability to participate in the government and decide its laws. Rome's upper classes, the social elite, were known as patricians. They were born to noble families and were often rich. All other citizens were known as plebeians or one of the common people.

Since the Republic's elected officials were not paid at first, a small group of wealthy patricians held these positions, and as a result, managed to dominate the government. The plebeians struggled against the patricians for more power, and in the 440s B.C., the plebians won an important victory.[1] They forced the patricians to publish the laws of Rome in a document that became known as the Twelve Tables. Now every Roman citizen could learn what the laws—and the punishments for breaking those rules—were.

Two groups of people were excluded from political affairs: all women, both patrician and plebeian, and slaves. Women were expected to remain at home and care for their families, while slaves were considered the property of their masters. As the Roman Empire grew, so did the number of captured enemy soldiers and rebellious residents of the provinces, who were enslaved and brought to Rome.[2]

The Assembly and Senate

During the Republic, Romans were involved in two important government bodies: the Assembly and the Senate. Every male citizen could attend one of four popular assemblies in Rome. At a meeting, which was held outdoors, he could vote on new laws and elect magistrates. Until 139 B.C., voting was done orally, and then secret ballots were used.

The Senate became very powerful during the Republic. Senators wrote new laws and took them to the assemblies for a vote. They also decided on policies for dealing with foreign nations, and at home they supervised financial matters. As the Republic grew in size, the Senate appointed governors to the newly added provinces and supervised their work. Senators were not elected directly by Rome's citizens. These men had previously served as magistrates, the Republic's government officials. All ex-magistrates automatically became senators for life. During the middle years of the Republic (from 264 B.C. to 134 B.C.), there were about three hundred senators.

Consuls and Other Magistrates

There were many types of magistrates in the Republic. Some did legal work, others worked with the Senate on legislation, and still others concerned themselves with

The buildings, squares, and temples in Rome known as the Forum were begun during the Republic and greatly expanded during the empire. The forum was the heart of every Roman town and city. This open square was surrounded by government buildings and temples. People came to the forum to vote, hear speeches, attend the law courts, read public notices, and discuss the issues of the day.

religious issues. There were at least two magistrates for each job because the Romans did not want power to be concentrated in the hands of one individual. All magistrates were elected by the assemblies, including the most powerful magistrates—the consuls.

When Rome became a republic in 509, two consuls, elected for one-year terms, replaced the king. They led the meetings of the Senate, and, more important, each one took charge of an army. In an emergency, the consuls stepped aside to make way for a dictator. The dictator could occupy

....

The members of the Roman senate debated many important issues in their chamber.

the position for six months at most. One of the Republic's most famous dictators was Lucius Quinctius Cincinnatus. According to legend, this hero left his farm to rescue his fellow citizens from hostile tribes in 458 B.C. He defeated the enemy and sixteen days later returned to his plow.

His immediate resignation of his absolute authority with the end of the crisis has often been cited as an example of outstanding leadership and service to the greater good. The government of the Roman Republic was a model of power sharing between the assemblies, the Senate, and the consuls. Each element was supposed to prevent the other two from gaining too much power.

The Government During the Empire

The old institutions of government changed under the emperor's dictatorship. Some of these institutions, like the assemblies, were not well adapted to the growing empire. By A.D. 14, at the end of Augustus' reign, there were at least 50 million people within the empire's borders, and many citizens lived too far from Rome to vote.[3] Although the assemblies continued to exist until about the third century A.D., they no longer represented the voice of the people.

Slavery was widespread and accepted in ancient Rome. Many slaves were prisoners of war. Slaves worked in businesses, in the fields, and in the home.

The Senate gave up a lot of its power to the emperor, but it seemed to grow in size along with the empire. By Constantine's time, there were two Senates, one in Constantinople and one in Rome, each with two thousand members! As for the consuls, they had little power.

Although a citizen had fewer opportunities to participate in the government during the Empire, Romans still valued their citizenship. In fact, the emperor often used citizenship as a reward to gain the loyalty and cooperation of those he conquered. As citizens of the Roman Empire, people in the provinces, such as Greeks, Spaniards, and Syrians, enjoyed the protection of Roman law. Since they were treated as equals, they were less likely to rebel.

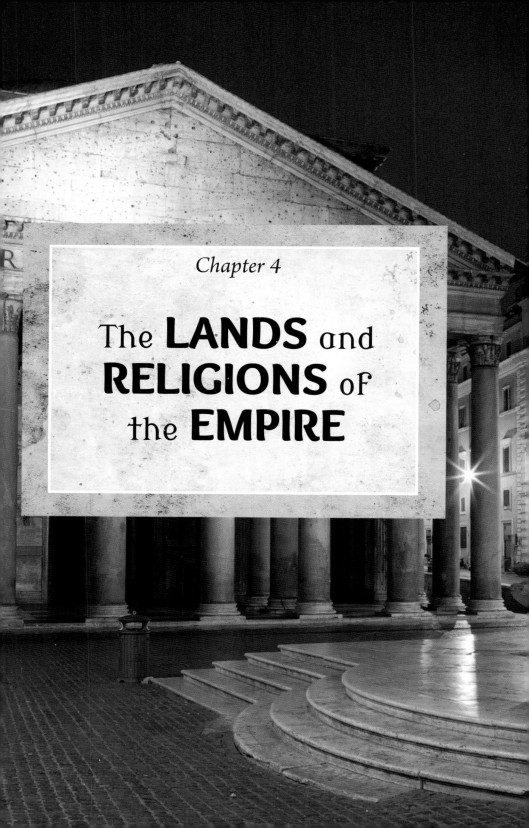

Chapter 4

The **LANDS** and **RELIGIONS** of the **EMPIRE**

The Roman Empire grew so much that it eventually touched on all the lands bordering the Mediterranean Sea. The land and its resources varied greatly from one province to the next, as did the people and their religions. Even as the empire was crumbling, however, Christianity was gradually spreading from east to west.

The Western Provinces

Ancient Italy was mostly an agricultural land. It would have been very difficult to farm the mountainous areas of the Alps in the north and the Apennines, a mountain range running down the length of the boot-shaped peninsula. But in the lowlands, Romans grazed cattle on large ranches and grew large crops of grains, such as millet, corn, wheat, and barley as well as peas and beans. Romans made their own wine and olive oil on the peninsula, and a good deal more was imported from Spain.

The Lands and Religions of the Empire

It took the Romans nearly two hundred years to make Spain a province. By then, Rome's influence could be seen in the network of roads linking Spain's cities and towns to that peninsula and the stone bridges crossing its rivers.[1] Both roads and rivers helped the Romans export Spanish products, including valuable gold, copper, and silver.

The southern regions of Gaul and Germany were dotted with urban centers, such as the city of Marseilles, a port on the Mediterranean Sea. In the more rural areas, grapes and olives were cultivated. North and west of the great plateau called the Massif Central, the heavy soil was devoted to farming, especially grains. There were large cattle ranches in Gaul and also in Britain. Although Britain did not enrich the empire in minerals, it grew enough corn to some-times feed the Roman troops as far away as those on the Rhine River in Germany.[2]

North Africa and the Eastern Mediterranean

The rich lands of north Africa lay between the Mediterranean Sea to the north, the Sahara Desert to the south, and Egypt to the east. Although the land sometimes needed irrigation when rainfall was low, the region supplied the Romans with an abundance of grain and olive oil. Not everyone farmed in this region, however. Great cities such as Carthage gave the empire lawyers, senators, and writers.

Agriculture flourished in the eastern Mediterranean. Grain was cultivated in coastal areas and in the fertile valley of the Nile River in Egypt. The surplus from Egypt's huge crops was shipped to the city of Rome to feed its people.[3] In Asia Minor, the sheep produced the best wool in the empire, which was exported to Italy.

The Roman Empire now encompassed a region of ancient civilizations. Judaea, now modern Israel and Palestine, was the birth-place of Judaism and, much later, of Christianity as well.

The State Religion

The ancient Romans, like the ancient Greeks, believed their world was shaped by many gods, who controlled everything from the rain needed for their crops to victory or defeat in battle. To gain their gods' goodwill, Romans built temples in their honor. Jupiter, their supreme god, was worshiped at a temple on one of the hills overlooking the Forum before the army went on a military expedition. Mars, the father of Romulus, Rome's founder, was at first the god of agriculture but later was worshipped as the god of war. At the Temple of Vesta, the goddess who guarded Roman homes, six young women stood guard over a sacred fire.

Gods and Goddesses

The Romans worshipped many gods and goddesses. Each god or goddess oversaw a part of Roman life.

JUNO

JUPITER

MARS

MERCURY

MINERVA

VENUS

Cupid—God of love; Venus's son.

Flora—Goddess of flowers and spring.

Juno—Queen of the gods; goddess of marriage and birth; wife to Jupiter.

Jupiter—King of the gods.

Mars—God of war; son of Jupiter and Juno.

Mercury—God of roads and travel; messenger of the gods; son of Jupiter.

Minerva—Goddess of wisdom; daughter of Jupiter.

Neptune—God of the sea; Jupiter's brother.

Saturn—God of fertility and planting; father of Jupiter and Neptune.

Sol—God of the sun.

Terra—Goddess of the earth.

Venus—Goddess of love and beauty; Cupid's mother.

Romans called their religion the "state religion" because when Rome was a city-state, the people thought that worshiping these gods would help to keep it safe.

Judaism

Unlike the Romans, the Jews of ancient Judaea believed in one supreme god. Before the rise of Christianity, they were nearly the only people who worshipped one god. During Roman times, their Temple, a large building in the city of Jerusalem, was their most important place of worship.

After the Romans conquered Judaea at the beginning of the first century B.C., they did not interfere with the Jews' worship. Many Jews resented Roman rule, however, and in A.D. 66, they rebelled. Titus forcibly ended the revolt in 70, before he became emperor, and destroyed the Temple. That year marked the beginning of the Diaspora, when Jews began leaving Judaea to live in communities scattered throughout the empire.

Christianity

In A.D. 28 or 29, a Jewish carpenter from Nazareth named Jesus began preaching about God in an area north of Jerusalem called Galilee. He claimed to have a relationship with God that was more personal than that experienced by traditional Jews. He preached that God's kingdom would soon be established on Earth. These teachings created both enthusiasm and fear among his listeners.[4]

When Jesus traveled south to Jerusalem, some Jewish leaders and Pontius Pilate, the Roman governor of Judaea, arranged to have him arrested and tried for treason. Jesus was nailed to a cross, a punishment that was given to rebels, and died. Soon afterward, his followers spread the word that he was not like other men, because they believed him to be the Son of God.

The earliest believers in Jerusalem thought Jesus' teachings were only for Jews. Paul of Tarsus, a Mediterranean city northwest of Judaea, preached that non-Jews could also become Christians. His view prevailed, and by A.D. 100, there were Christian communities in most important cities of the vast Roman Empire.[5]

But the Roman Empire under the emperor Nero persecuted early Christians for their beliefs. When a huge and destructive fire burned in Rome in A.D. 64, many

This statue of Jesus Christ as the Good Shepherd is signifcant because it was made in secret at a time when Christianity was still generally forbidden.

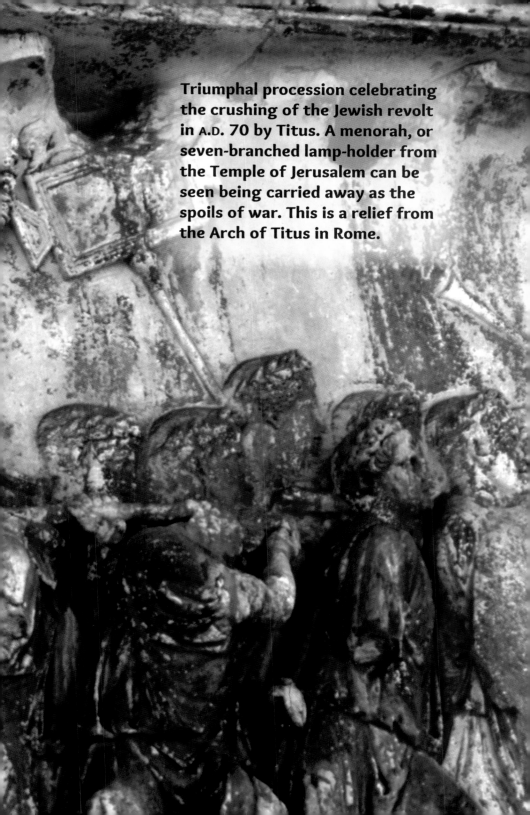

Triumphal procession celebrating the crushing of the Jewish revolt in A.D. 70 by Titus. A menorah, or seven-branched lamp-holder from the Temple of Jerusalem can be seen being carried away as the spoils of war. This is a relief from the Arch of Titus in Rome.

The remains of the temple of Vesta, in the Roman Forum. In Roman mythology, Vesta was the goddess of hearth and home.

Romans placed the blame on Nero, a violent man who had murdered both his mother and his wife. Nero blamed the fire on the Christian community in the city of Rome. He rounded up as many Christians as he could and killed them. Christians continued to be persecuted by the Romans under a series of emperors. Finally, in 313, the emperor Constantine announced that Christianity would be legally permitted in the empire.

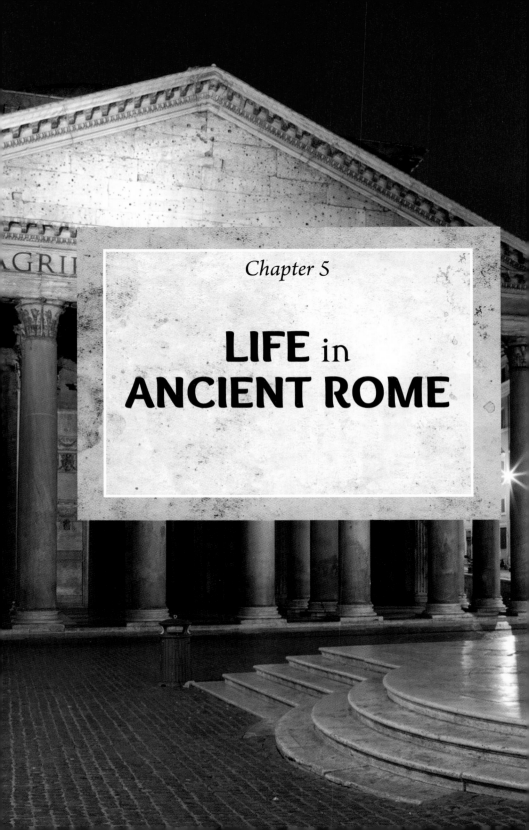

Chapter 5

LIFE in ANCIENT ROME

Early in the morning of August 24, A.D. 79, the residents of Pompeii, on the west coast of Italy, felt the earth shake. Then they heard a thunderclap as Mount Vesuvius, a nearby volcano, erupted, spewing hot lava and ash into the sky.[1] Poisonous fumes and thousands of tons of ash settled over the small town.[2] The fumes and ash killed those who did not manage to escape. But all the ash that helped to destroy Pompeii also preserved it, leaving an amazingly detailed picture of everyday life in a Roman town. In the ancient ruins are the remains of shops where people worked, houses where they lived, public baths where they went to visit with friends, and theaters where they were entertained. The rhythms of life in Pompeii, which ended so suddenly, were repeated in countless Roman towns and cities.

Plaster casts of people killed at the ancient Roman city of Pompeii, which was destroyed and buried during the eruption of Mount Vesuvius in A.D. 79. In time, the bodies buried under volcanic ash at Pompeii and nearby sites decomposed. Modern excavators poured plaster into the void left behind in the ash, making casts of the victims in their last moments.

Family Life

In ancient Rome, marriage partners were usually chosen for young men and women by older relatives. If marrying for the first time, they were likely to be teenagers. A bride might be only thirteen years old.

Weddings were celebrated at the bride's house. After a banquet, the groom would pretend to take the bride out of her mother's arms. Then, in a rowdy procession, the wedding celebrants joked with the couple and escorted them to the groom's house, the bride's new home.[3]

Romans usually lived only with their children rather than in an extended family. Parents tended to be strict because they believed that it helped young people grow strong enough to handle the problems of adult life. In an essay on raising children, Seneca the Younger, a Roman philosopher, wrote, "We must be careful not to let them have fits of anger, but," he added, "we must also be careful not to stifle their individual personalities."[4]

Most parents thought play should be a part of growing up. Babies had rattles, and older children played with marbles and dolls. Of course, parents were more concerned about their children's education than about their toys.

Education

During the early years of the Republic, fathers taught their sons how to read, write, and use weapons. By about the third century B.C., wealthy and middle-class families sent children between the ages of seven and eleven to an elementary school to learn reading, writing, and arithmetic. School was often held outside under the awning of a shop. A cloth screen might shut out the distractions in the street, but not the noise.[5]

A girl's education ended at age eleven, but boys went on to study Latin and Greek literature. A few boys from wealthy families prepared for a career in politics or law by studying with a *rhetor*, who taught the art of public speaking. At the age of sixteen, the son of a patrician family often became a senator's apprentice for a year.

Food and Drink

A Roman family's diet depended on their social status. Those with little money ate wheat, which was probably boiled because the poor usually did not have ovens for baking. They also ate beans and leeks, but meat was a luxury. In modest homes, cheap wine and vinegar mixed with water were common beverages. Romans of all classes disapproved of drinking wine without water. Romans used milk to make cheese, but they did not drink it. They thought only uncivilized people drank milk!

As can be seen in the ruins of Pompeii, homes of the rich usually had big, fancy paintings, know as frescoes, on the walls.

The Romans decorated their homes with painted murals and sculpture. This Roman couple chose to have their likenesses portrayed on the wall of their house. This portrait was found in the main room of a home attached to a bakery in Pompeii.

The wealthy drank wine and ate a wide variety of meats, vegetables, and fish. An invitation from the poet Martial to a friend offers a glimpse of a middle-class Roman's taste and hospitality: "If you are worried about a lonely dinner at home, Toranius, you can come share your hunger with me. If you are accustomed to an appetizer, you won't be disappointed; there will be cheap Cappadocian lettuce and strong leeks and tuna fish garnished with sliced eggs. . . . We will also have a small sausage served on a bed of white grits [a boiled wheat dish] and pale beans and red bacon."[6]

Clothing and Shelter

Men and women wore togas in early Rome, but eventually togas were worn by male Roman citizens only. The toga was a heavy, expensive garment made from a large piece of white woolen fabric about eighteen feet long. The fabric was draped over the body in a complicated way that was difficult for a man to arrange by himself. Cincinnatus, the great Roman who according to legend became a dictator for sixteen days, always had his wife, Racilia, help him put on his toga. Eventually, a man wore his toga over a tunic, a straight, short-sleeved garment tied at the waist.

When women stopped wearing togas, they wore tunics covered by *stola*, long full dresses with a colored border around the neckline. Children and slaves wore tunics.

Romans who lived in towns often lived in stone houses built for single families. The most common style was an atrium house built around a central open area, which at times had no roof. In cities with the largest populations, such as Rome, many people owned or rented apartments in a private house, above a shop, or in a large apartment building.

Romans in Pompeii are entertained in their home by a traveling musician playing a lyre.

The foundation of an oval-shaped house still stands today.

Most of the farmland in Italy was divided into large tracts that were owned by the wealthy. On these estates the landowner and his family often lived in a large building complex, called a villa, which had enough living space for farm workers and even for the livestock. Families with small farms and modest incomes lived in simple huts.

Roman Recreation

Romans enjoyed a variety of entertainment, from literary plays to violent combat. The combat, which were called "games," took place in large, open-air amphitheaters, which looked like today's football stadiums. These deadly sword fights between gladiators, specially trained men who wore helmets and shields, were very popular. Some of these gladiators became celebrities, like the one who inspired someone to scrawl on a wall in Pompeii, "Celadus,

These women wear togas. Early on both men and women wore togas.

the Thracian, makes all the girls sigh."[7]
People also liked to watch fights between a
variety of wild animals. On the opening day
of the enormous Colosseum, an amphitheater in the city of Rome that held about
forty-five thousand spectators, five thousand
animals waited their turn in cages.

The most popular form of entertainment
in ancient Rome was the chariot race. Men
raced teams of chariots, each one pulled by
four horses, around a U-shaped arena. The
races took place in a building called a circus,
which had tiers of seats rising away from the
arena. In the Circus Maximus in Rome, up
to 250,000 people could cheer for their
favorite team—the red, blue, white, or green.

The ancient Romans also liked to go to
plays. In Pompeii, theatergoers could watch
a comedy in a large, open-air building.
Poetry lovers could go to the Odeon, a small
theater with a roof, to hear a poet read his
latest verses.

Wine was an essential of the Roman diet. It was sold by the cup-measure at wine-merchants and available at taverns.

Combat between gladiators. These lethal games were popular all over the Empire where amphitheaters and scenes like this one were widely found.

Public baths offered yet another place for Romans to enjoy themselves. People of all social classes could go daily to exercise, soak in the warm water, and socialize with friends. The philosopher Seneca the Younger, who lived above a bathhouse, found the noise distracting. "When the more muscular types are exercising and swinging about lead weights in their hands, and when they are straining themselves . . . I hear groans," he complained.[8]

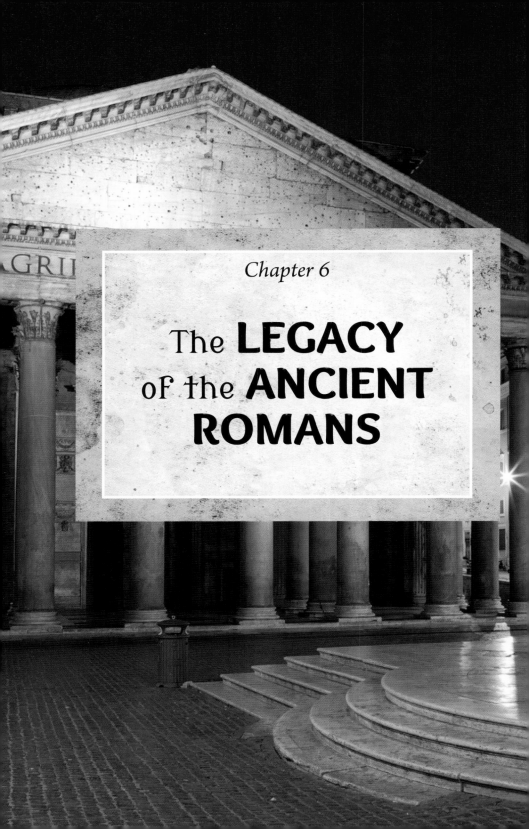

Chapter 6

The **LEGACY** of the **ANCIENT ROMANS**

The ancient Romans have influenced modern life around the world in countless ways, from the governments that serve the people to the languages they speak, the calendars they keep, and the buildings they construct.

A Government of Checks and Balances

The United States government, with its executive branch headed by the president, and its legislature made up of two bodies, the Senate and the House of Representatives, is based in part on the organization of the governing bodies of ancient Roman Republic. The United States Senate was directly inspired by the Senate of ancient Rome. Most modern democracies are organized in the same way, so that one branch of government does not become too powerful.

Language and Literature

The ancient Romans spoke Latin. As their empire expanded, that language replaced local languages in many of the provinces. Five languages evolved directly from Latin: French, Spanish, Italian, Portuguese, and Romanian. As a group they are called the Romance languages because their parent language was the language spoken by the Romans. Although English grew out of a different family of languages, many English words, including art, beauty, justice, space, and time have Latin origins.

Ancient Rome's greatest works of literature are still read today in the original Latin and in translation. Many of these works were written around the time of Augustus' peaceful reign, including the works of Virgil (70–19 B.C.), who is viewed today as ancient Rome's greatest poet.[1] Virgil's long epic poem the *Aeneid*, which

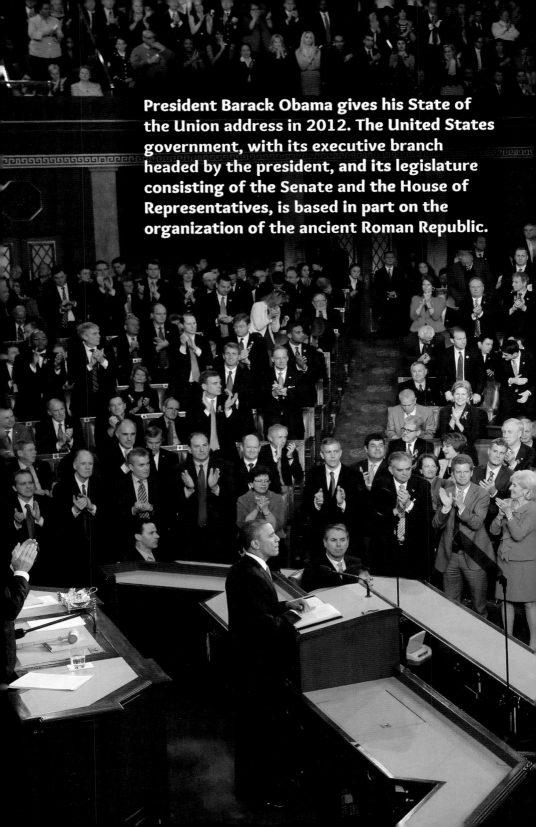

President Barack Obama gives his State of the Union address in 2012. The United States government, with its executive branch headed by the president, and its legislature consisting of the Senate and the House of Representatives, is based in part on the organization of the ancient Roman Republic.

The great wooden horse loomed at the gates of Troy after the Greek besiegers had apparently withdrawn. The Trojans, curious brought it into their city. At night, the Greeks emerged from the wooden horse and captured the city. This is one of the stories that Virgil relates in the *Aeneid*.

celebrates the achievements of the empire, is a literary classic. Ovid (43 B.C.–A.D. 17) is known today for his often irreverent poems, which display what modern readers might call "attitude." That may explain why

Augustus banished Ovid to Tomis on the coast of the Black Sea.

Another writer who was banished and then executed was Cicero (106–43 B.C.), considered by many to have been Rome's greatest public speaker and essayist. He was devoted to preserving the Republic and was not afraid to speak out against anyone he considered a threat. Among his famous speeches were the fourteen he delivered against Marc Antony, which Cicero paid for with his life. Eight hundred of Cicero's letters survive today. They are a valuable source of information on ancient Rome for historians.

The Julian Calendar

Although Julius Caesar is best known for his military genius, his most lasting contribution to modern times was a complicated assortment of changes that he made to the Roman calendar in 46 B.C.

The Pantheon is a prime example of classical Roman architecture. The inscription on the facade refers to M. Agrippa, the Pantheon's builder who was a friend and colleague of Augustus.

The Julian calendar was made up of cycles of three 365-day years, followed by one year of 366 days, or leap year. It is the calendar still in use today. The reason for Caesar's changes was that the calendar had lost its connection with the seasons, and Caesar's alterations meant that summer would always fall in June and winter in December.

Architecture and Engineering

Some of Rome's greatest works in architecture and engineering are still standing and have inspired generations of engineers, builders, and designers. The Pont du Gard still spans the Gard River in graceful arches outside of the French city of Nîmes. It is a beautiful example of the ingenious aqueducts built by the Romans to bring fresh water from miles away into the cities for drinking and bathing.

The Legacy of the Ancient Romans

Amphitheaters were found throughout the Roman empire, including this one in Ephesus, Turkey.

The influence of Rome's classical architecture can be seen in the United States Capitol Building, for which construction began in 1793. Thomas Jefferson wanted Congress housed in a replica of an ancient Roman temple.

The Legacy of the Ancient Romans

In the city of Rome, the Pantheon, a temple to all Roman gods, looks very much as it did two thousand years ago, when Hadrian rebuilt it. This masterpiece is crowned by a dome measuring 142 feet across—the widest dome in the world until the twentieth century.[2] The influence of Rome's classical architecture is reflected in many American buildings, including the United States Capitol building in the city of Washington, D.C., and at Monticello, the home Thomas Jefferson designed for himself in Virginia.

The ancient Romans have left traces of their civilization and empire all over the continent of Europe and beyond. Visitors to northern England can see the remnants of Hadrian's Wall in the countryside. In Turkey, the ruins of a Roman amphitheater sit just a few miles from the ancient city of Ephesus. The largest amphitheater in the empire was the Colosseum. It could fit up to 50,000 people at once. In Libya, tourists can walk through entire neighborhoods of the ancient Roman city of Leptis Magna.

Most modern people do not celebrate war as the Romans did—thank goodness! But they share many other elements of ancient Roman culture. Health and fitness, literature, humor, good food, and great architecture are very much appreciated today, just as they were during Hadrian's time. Modern people are also concerned about the rights of citizens. We owe the ancient Romans, and the Greeks before them, a great debt of gratitude for passing down to us their concept of citizenship.

TIMELINE

509 B.C.—The Romans defeat the Etruscan king Tarquin the Proud and establish the Republic.

c. 440 B.C.—The Twelve Tables, the Republic's laws, are published

264–241 B.C.—First Punic War: Rome defeats Carthage, in north Africa, and adds islands of Sicily, Sardinia, and Corsica.

218–202 B.C.—Second Punic War: Carthaginian general Hannibal marches from Spain to Rome but is defeated by the Roman Commander Publius Scipio Africanus at the Battle of Zama.

146 B.C.—Romans destroy Carthage, which later becomes a Roman colony; Greece becomes a Roman province.

48 B.C.—Julius Caesar defeats Pompey and two years later begins his rule of Rome.

44 B.C.—Caesar is assassinated, and civil war erupts.

31 B.C.—Octavian, Caesar's great-nephew, defeats Marc Antony and Cleopatra to become sole ruler of Rome.

27 B.C. –A.D. 14—Octavian/Augustus becomes the first emperor of the Roman Empire. His peaceful reign ushers in the Pax Romana, or peace of Rome, in which Roman and Greek culture spread throughout the empire.

A.D. 14—Tiberius succeeds his stepfather, Augustus, as emperor.

A.D. 30—Jesus of Nazareth is crucified.

A.D. 43—The emperor Claudius begins the conquest of Britain.

A.D. 70—The emperor Titus crushes the Jewish revolt, and the Jewish Diaspora begins.

A.D. 79—Mount Vesuvius erupts, destroying the Roman cities of Pompeii and Herculaneum.

A.D. 98–A.D. 117—Under Trajan's rule, the Roman Empire is at its greatest size.

A.D. 122—Hadrian builds defensive wall across northern border of Britain.

c. A.D. 125—Hadrian rebuilds the Pantheon, originally constructed in 27 B.C.

A.D. 286—Diocletian divides the empire into eastern and western parts.

A.D. 330—Constantine moves the capital to Constantinople.

A.D. 476—The Goth king Odoacer removes Romulus Augustulus as ruler, bringing an end to Roman rule of the western Roman Empire.

GLOSSARY

A.D.—An abbreviation for the Latin *anno Domini,* meaning "in the year of our Lord." Used for a measurement of time, a.d. indicates the number of years since the supposed birthdate of Christ.

amphitheater—A large stadium-like structure with rows of seats in tiers.

aqueducts—Large arch-shaped structures built to carry water directly to Rome from an outside source.

barbarians—A word used by Greeks and Romans to describe foreigners.

B.C.—Before Christ. Used for a measurement of time, b.c. indicates the number of years before the supposed birthdate of Christ.

citizen—In ancient Rome, a citizen was originally a freeborn man.

civilization—A kind of culture marked by a high level of organization in government and religion. Trade, writing, and art are all a part of civilization.

Colosseum—A huge stadium in Rome.

column—A slender upright structure used in architecture to support a roof, an upper story, or the top part of a wall.

consul—One of the two high-ranking officials who headed the ancient Roman government.

democracy—A government in which citizens rule and share power.

dictator—One who has absolute power over a country.

emperor—The ruler or leader of an empire.

empire—A nation and the country it rules.

forum—A marketplace in ancient Rome.

gladiator—A specially trained slave during Roman times who fought with wild animals.

patrician—Aristocratic, well-born members of Roman society who held important positions in government.

plebeian—A citizen of ancient Rome. In the early days of the Republic, plebeians had little say in government.

republic—Any government that is not headed by a king or queen. In a republic, the powers rest with the people.

Glossary

senate—A group who advised the consuls of ancient Rome.

slave—Man, woman, or child who is owned by another person in the same way as a piece of property, usually to do work of some kind.

tribe—A social group held together by family ties, geography, or custom.

CHAPTER NOTES

Chapter 1. CAESAR'S DECISION

1. Charles Freeman, *The World of the Romans* (New York: Oxford University Press, 1993), p. 19.
2. Chris Scarre, *The Penguin Historical Atlas of Ancient Rome* (London: Penguin Books, 1995), p. 30.
3. Quoted in Michael Grant, *The Twelve Caesars* (New York: Charles Scribner, 1975), p. 32.

Chapter 2. FROM REPUBLIC TO EMPIRE

1. Charles Freeman, *The World of the Romans* (New York: Oxford University Press, 1993), p. 20.
2. Michael Grant, *The Twelve Caesars* (New York: Charles Scribner, 1975), p. 33.
3. Quoted in Moses Hadas, ed., *A History of Rome from Its Origins to 529 A.D. As Told by the Roman Historians* (New York: Doubleday, 1956), p. 80.
4. Grant, p. 50.
5. Freeman, p. 6.
6. Chester G. Starr, *The Ancient Romans* (New York: Oxford University Press, 1971), p. 27.

7. Freeman, p. 65.
8. Ibid., p. 174.

Chapter 3. THE REPUBLICAN GOVERNMENT AND ITS PEOPLE

1. Charles Freeman, *The World of the Romans* (New York: Oxford University Press, 1993), p. 7.
2. Jo-Ann Shelton, *As the Romans Did: A Sourcebook in Roman Social History* (New York: Oxford University Press, 1988), p. 168.
3. Lesley Adkins and Roy A. Adkins, *Handbook to Life in Ancient Rome* (New York: Oxford University Press, 1998), p. 341.

Chapter 4. THE LANDS AND RELIGIONS OF THE EMPIRE

1. Chris Scarre, *The Penguin Historical Atlas of Ancient Rome* (London: Penguin Books, 1995), p. 84.
2. Tim Cornell and John Matthews, *Atlas of the Roman World* (New York: Facts on File, 1982), p. 134.
3. Scarre, p. 74.
4. Charles Freeman, *The World of the Romans* (New York: Oxford University Press, 1993), p. 85.
5. Chester G. Starr, *The Ancient Romans* (New York: Oxford University Press, 1971), p. 187.

Chapter 5. LIFE IN ANCIENT ROME

1. Robert Etienne, *Pompeii: The Day a City Died*, trans. Caroline Palmer (New York: Harry Abrams, 1992), inside cover.
2. Charles Freeman, *The World of the Romans* (New York: Oxford University Press, 1993), p. 132.
3. Florence Dupont, *Daily Life in Ancient Rome,* trans. Christopher Woodall (Oxford: Blackwell, 1992), p. 109.
4. Quoted in Jo-Ann Shelton, *As the Romans Did: A Sourcebook in Roman Social History* (New York: Oxford University Press, 1988), p. 31.
5. Jérôme Carcopino, *Daily Life in Ancient Rome: The People and the City at the Height of the Empire*, ed. Henry T. Rowell, trans. E. O. Lorimer (New Haven, Conn.: Yale University Press, 1968), p. 105.
6. Quoted in Jo-Ann Shelton, p. 83.
7. Freeman, p. 73.
8. Shelton, p. 314.

Chapter 6. THE LEGACY OF THE ANCIENT ROMANS

1. Charles Freeman, *The World of the Romans* (New York: Oxford University Press, 1993), p. 187.
2. Ibid., p. 88.

FURTHER READING

BOOKS

Corbishley, Mike. *Ancient Rome*. New York: Chelsea House, 2007.

Decker, Zilah. *Ancient Rome: Archaeology Unlocks the Secrets of Rome's Past*. Washington, D.C.: National Geographic, 2007.

Innes, Brian. *Ancient Roman Myths*. New York: Gareth Stevens Pub., 2010.

Mellor, Ronald, and Marni McGee. *The Ancient Roman World*. New York: Oxford University Press, 2004.

Nardo, Don. *Women of Ancient Rome*. San Diego: Lucent Books, 2003.

Pistone, Nicholas, Giovanni Di Pasquale, and Matilde Bardi. *Art and Culture of Ancient Rome*. New York: Rosen Pub., 2010.

Schomp, Virignia. *The Ancient Romans*. New York: Marshall Cavendish Benchmark, 2009.

Tames, Richard. *Ancient Roman Children*. Chicago: Heinemann Library, 2003.

Thorne, James. *Julius Caesar: Conqueror and Dictator*. New York: Rosen Publishing Group, 2003.

INTERNET ADDRESSES

Ancient Rome: Odyssey Online
from Emory University
  <http://carlos.emory.edu/ODYSSEY/ROME/
  homepg.html>

Rome: Republic to Empire: Barbara F. McManus,
The College of New Rochelle
  <http://www.vroma.org/~bmcmanus/romanpages.
  html>

INDEX